A Mother's Struggle 3:1

A Mother's Struggle
3:1

Apostle E.C. Friar

Copyright © 2021 E.C. Friar.

All rights reserved. No part of this publication may be reproduced, distributed, or transmitted in any form or by any means, including photocopying, recording, or other electronic or mechanical methods, without the prior written permission of the publisher, except in the case of brief quotations embodied in critical reviews and certain other noncommercial uses permitted by copyright law. For permission requests, write to the publisher, addressed "Attention: Permissions Coordinator," at the address below.

ISBN: 978-1-7363137-0-1

Unless otherwise noted, all Scriptures are taken from the KING JAMES VERSION (KJV): KING JAMES VERSION, public domain.

This is a work of creative nonfiction. The events are portrayed to the best of the author's memory. While all the stories in this book are true, some names and identifying details have been changed to protect the privacy of the people involved.

Book production by Marvin D. Cloud.

Printed in the United States of America.

First printing edition 2020.

Apostle E.C. Friar
www.standstillandknow.com

*I dedicate this book to others living with
the loss of a child.*

Acknowledgments

Special thanks to my husband, Darrell Sr., and our children, Darrell, Patresia, Crystal, and T.J.

I also thank my parents, John and Martha, my sister, Roshanda, and mother-in-law, Willie Mae.

To our family and friends, thank you for your loving support and encouragement through this difficult time and down through the years.

May God continue to bless and keep you all.

Introduction

There is no pain like the death of a child. No enemy can inflict more hurt than watching the lifeless body of an offspring laying in a casket. Many young people die because of disease, accident, suicide, drugs or gang violence. Yet each year, more women in particular and men in general, become desensitized to intentional deaths that take place in the womb.

Norma Leah Nelson McCorvey died in 2017. I understand if your response was "who's that?" That's because she was better known as "Jane Roe," the plaintiff in Roe v. Wade whereby the U.S. Supreme Court ruled in 1973 that individual state laws banning abortion were unconstitutional.

That decision legally opened the doors for women to abort an estimated 61,628,584 babies' lives, according to National Right to Life. I was one of those women.

While I can't speak for anyone else, it would be a lie if I said each time was an easy decision. It wasn't.

I will tell no one I accepted the adage "Out of sight, out of mind." I didn't, and they weren't.

And then, there are others who have lost a child prematurely, with no rhyme or reason, while the child was sound asleep. According to the Center for Disease Control and Prevention (CDC), "About 3,600 babies in the United States die unexpectedly each year. A thorough investigation is necessary to learn what caused these deaths. Sudden unexpected infant deaths include sudden infant death syndrome (SIDS), accidental suffocation in a sleeping environment, and other deaths from unknown causes. Although the SUID rate has declined since 1990s, significant racial and ethnic differences continue."

However, nothing could prepare me for the sudden death of our infant daughter as she laid by my side. Was God punishing me for past sins? Did He decide to take a child I loved because I apparently had no love for the ones I aborted? After past indiscretions, did I deserve to be a mother?

These and other questions whirled through my mind as I wrestled with my sanity and questioned my God. So when I say *I know how you feel*, it's not rhetoric, and it does not come from a place of hollow words without substance. I know how you feel. I've been there and I have the scars to prove it.

Regardless of my experience and the thrust upon me expertise in the matter, I'm not here to teach you about the stages of grief. I'm here to tell you, there is a brighter day ahead. I'm not saying you forget, but you get better instead of bitter. And it's all with the help of the same God whose wisdom and power you questioned and rejected early in the process.

You get to sing again. You get the opportunity to love once more. As difficult as it might seem now, you get to live again.

I wrote *A Mother's Struggle 3:1* from my vantage point, but I didn't write it for me. I wrote it for the countless number of mothers (and fathers) who must deal with the loss of a child. Know that you are not alone. The pages of this book contain encouragement and entitlement. They will show you that no matter how dark the hour may appear, daylight is coming.

The Psalmist tells us and I found this to be true: "For his anger endureth but a moment; in his favour is life: weeping may endure for a night, but joy cometh in the morning" (Psalm 30:5).

Chapter One

The Lord is my light and my salvation; whom shall I fear? the Lord is the strength of my life; of whom shall I be afraid?

—**Psalm 27:1**

Everyone has a testimony of where they've been and what God has brought them through. However, shame often hides the true testimony. It may help someone else get delivered. The enemy doesn't want your story told. Regardless of negative outcomes, under eyed stares, or crooked frowns, here is my story.

For years I'd struggled with and looked to find love in places where I couldn't find any. I wound up in the arms of man after man. I could say it was because I didn't have any structure in the home, or I grew up without a father. Those excuses don't apply. I wanted something I felt was missing in my life.

At age 22, I became pregnant with my first child by a man named Peter. I was excited, afraid, and anxious. I never thought of disposing the special person growing inside of me. I'd been taught it was wrong to abort. "Thou shalt not kill" was a command from God taught in our Christian home and in the church Sunday school class. I wasn't obeying God, but I knew abortion wasn't an option.

The relationship with Peter led me further away from my family because they considered him a bad boy of sorts. I would sometimes sleep on the floor at the homes of friends and family members to be with him. I was now pregnant with no money and we had no place to go. We slept in an abandoned apartment complex one night. He went out to get money the only way he knew how, but he kept coming up short.

One day, I came to my senses. Like the prodigal son in the Bible, I thought, *I can go home to my parent's house. I don't have to live this way.* They gladly welcomed me back, but I had concern for my unborn child's father having to survive without food or shelter. I asked my parents if he could stay with us for a while, and they agreed under the condition that we slept in separate rooms.

The plan worked good for a while, then we got extremely comfortable. We would somehow end up with each other each night. Either he was in my room or I was in his room. Peter worked part time and my dad helped him get a car, but our relationship was toxic. We argued and fought all the time. Peter was a couple of years older than me, but he had no experience with life outside of prison. He'd spent many years behind bars as a teenager for grand theft auto and fighting. He was a highly skilled boxer. Even though I gave him a run for his money, so to speak, he never physically hurt me. We went back and forth with this type of behavior until our daughter, Tina, was born and my parents were fed up. He had a car and a job but no longer wanted to abide by the rules of the house and he left. We still dated, but we no longer lived under the same roof.

When I was six months pregnant, a close friend of mine needed a ride one day to the Houston Housing Authority. She and I had an extremely long wait for her appointment. She looked at me and asked, "Why don't you apply for assistance while we're here?" I filled out the application but had no idea they would call me in for an interview that same day. They called the number I had pulled from the machine to show my place in line. The lady asked several questions about me and my income, but the last thing she asked was, "Why do you need help?"

I said, "Well, I'm pregnant by a white man and my parents said they'll kick me out once this baby is born." The caseworker looked up from her stack of files and paperwork as if she'd never heard such a sad story. It was a lie which rolled off my tongue. I had not rehearsed it and when I exited the building I said, "Wow, that was a good one!" I received Housing assistance six months later, and we moved into our first apartment. Tina had turned three months old by then, and we seemed to be doing good.

Eventually, the relationship with Peter failed after the authorities jailed him for 30 days for giving the police a false name. I then entered a brief relationship with Charles, who lived in the apartments across from us. We had loads of fun, but there was an altercation between him and his brother after I mentioned his brother made a pass at me. They fought in his living room while I hid in the bathroom and prayed. I heard his brother threatening to kill me. This relationship was a secret, but it produced another pregnancy which ended in abortion.

I tried to cover up the betrayal of infidelity in Peter's absence by using this method to resolve the situation. I thought by cutting Charles off and getting rid of the evidence, everything would be good. Charles and his family did not go along with the program. This would have been his second child, and he wanted me to go through with it, but my history with Peter wouldn't allow me to move on. I started the relationship with Charles because I thought I was finished with Peter and his childish games. Charles and his sisters eventually ratted me out, which caused Peter to leave me. Several months passed and over time, Peter and I still had moments of casual intimacy, even though he now lived with another woman. Before long, I was pregnant again. I didn't have a stable relationship, job, or money. To top it off, the lady he lived with claimed to his family that she was pregnant. When I heard about it, I thought, *I'm not having a baby at the same time as her.*

I saved money gifted by family and friends until I had enough gathered to do away with the pregnancy. This pregnancy was different because now, I was almost five months along. It was difficult to get the money together because they based the procedure costs on the trimester. I went into the clinic and paid for the abortion, not knowing what was about to happen. I didn't understand exactly what this baby would experience.

My aunt took my daughter and I into her home for about a week and cared for us because the clinic had advised me not to be alone during this process. The people at the clinic stated there were two parts to this procedure. They first impacted and lined the vaginal walls with seaweed like material, which helped detach the fetus from the uterus. Then I was to return the next day for the complete fetal extraction. Depression took its toll, but I soothed it by drowning the sorrow in alcohol. I begged and pleaded for God's forgiveness, but never felt forgiven. I bore a guilty conscience, and I moved on to even more failed relationships. This behavior went on for quite some time until I met Anthony. I believed he was the true love who came to rescue me. I thought it was real this time, but we married and separated within six months. We had different views of marriage. Anthony was unpredictable; I never knew what came next. We were a blended family with two children. He had a son, and I had a daughter. We all shared the two-bedroom apartment where my daughter and I lived prior to the union.

He worked hard, but he was an alcoholic, which made him quite reckless and irresponsible. Anthony and I started new jobs around the same time, and we had to put a week in the hole before we got paid. We had the children to care for and little to no money. There was one can of corn and one can of green beans in the pantry and only one package of meat in the freezer. Anthony got paid first, plus he was a truck driver, and his salary was higher than mine. He got paid and bought a new car instead of taking care of home first.

He decided without discussion, we would sleep on the floor at his parents' house until we got paid again because the lights were about to be disconnected. This disregard for our family was not acceptable, and he had to go. I packed his things and asked him to leave because my daughter and I would not live like that. The new car was unnecessary because his old one only needed a fuel pump. The disregard of my feelings and our family seemed unforgivable. I couldn't wrap my head around such a stupid decision. Once he and his son moved out,

I reverted to the old patterned behaviors of drinking and sleeping around with various partners.

We tried repeatedly to make that marriage work, but Anthony and I seemed to have grown too far apart to repair the damage. We didn't trust each other anymore, and love wasn't enough to keep us together. He had been with other women and I'd been with other men. The adultery was an ongoing event, often excused by the wrong committed during the six-month courtship and marriage.

He was abusive, especially when he was drunk. He would punch me with all his might with a smile on his face. Don't get me wrong, I was no angel, but I didn't deserve that from anyone. The demeaning things I said to provoke him were horrible and I will never repeat them under any circumstances. No reason is good enough to warrant abuse, but in hindsight, I could have avoided some pain by keeping my mouth shut. Even though we couldn't make things work, we remained married but separated for seven years as my life continued to spiral out of control.

Chapter Two

When the wicked, even mine enemies and my foes, came upon me to eat up my flesh, they stumbled and fell.

—Psalm 27:2

My daughter had turned five years when I met a guy who swept me off my feet. I was head over heels for him and again, I knew he was the one for me. We were both guests at an anniversary party that took place in a hole in the wall café. On one side there were pool tables and on the other side was a large bar, a huge dance floor, and lots of tables with chairs and the DJ booth. Peter's cousin who was also an old high school friend of mine invited me. I got bored fast, and I created a game called "pull me a ni**a."

After scoping the club, I spotted this tall handsome guy, and I told my friend, "I'm going to pull him tonight." She and I made a bet. I crept toward the pool tables where he and some other guys stood. It was customary whenever you wanted to play the next round of pool, to put a quarter on the table. I put my money down and waltzed my way onto the dance floor for the electric slide. I looked over at him and we made eye contact. I danced more seductively because I knew he was watching. It was now my turn to shoot pool. Women would play against women and the men against men. The tables were close, and I kept accidently bumping into him. He laughed but said nothing. I'd noticed he and I had a mutual friend named Jack. When the guy disappeared to the restroom, I asked Jack, "Who's your friend?"

He said, "You know him from the neighborhood. That's John L."

"I don't know him. Why don't you introduce me to him?"

Jack was reluctant because he knew John L. was involved with someone I knew well. Nevertheless, when John L. returned from the restroom, Jack introduced us and left the area abruptly because he didn't want to be in the middle of any confusion.

John L. offered to buy me a drink, but we didn't talk much. I went back over to my friend's table, and suddenly the lights popped on because the club was about to close. My friend and I walked toward the door, then Jack and John L. stopped us. I asked him again, "What's your name?" and he told me his nickname.

I demanded, "What's the name your momma gave you?"

He blurted out his full name and included three ways to contact him. The guys asked us out for breakfast, but my friend wasn't interested in Jack and she wanted me to drop her off at home. John L. and Jack rode to the club together, therefore he had to take Jack home, which was located next door to my grandparents' house.

Jack and I grew up together playing in the yard, but John L. lived a couple of streets over. We all attended the same schools and had mutual friends, but I didn't remember John L. at all. After I dropped my friend off, we met up and John L. followed me back to my new apartment.

We were hungry, and I told him not to worry about stopping for food, we could eat at my place. It was funny because I hadn't made groceries and the fridge was bare, but I found something he enjoyed. I took some bologna and fried it in a pan with toasted hot dog buns, then added mayo, lettuce, and tomatoes with an enormous glass of red Kool-Aid. I watched him eat two of those sandwiches and we laughed all night. I didn't want to blow it this time. I'd decided no sex on the first date. Jack tried it, but it was not happening. He got dressed and cuddled with me all night.

He told me from the start he had a lady, but he'd never been married. It was crazy because I was still legally married. About three months into the courtship, I found out I was pregnant. I was catching some deep feelings for John L. and figured it was time to discuss his relationship with the other woman. Through a lengthy conversation about the lady, I discovered I knew her. Rebecca lived across the street from my grandparents and we were childhood friends. I felt bad about loving him, especially after I found out about Rebecca. I tried to convince him to help me get out of the pregnancy, but he wouldn't give me any money. My conscience didn't bother me as long as he hid her from me. However, this recent information affected my decision about having a baby and the relationship with John L. I didn't want to hurt her but I know we did.

I borrowed money from relatives to undergo the third abortion. It would be the last time because it was the worst of all. I laid on that cold, hard table. The anesthesia hadn't taken effect yet, and the doctor came in and immediately started the procedure.

He asked, "Are you ready?"

He didn't wait for my response. I could hear the loud machine which acted as a vacuum with strong suctioning.

I yelled out, "Wait! I can feel that! You're hurting me!"

The doctor continued the procedure and ignored my cry for help. Instead, he scolded the nurses for not restraining me properly. At that moment, I vowed to God I would never do that again, if he would let me live. What an oxymoron; I laid there and begging for my life, while destroying another.

John L. had keys to my apartment and he let himself in to find me asleep mid day with the clinic bracelet still attached to my wrist.

He asked, "What have you done?"

I didn't have to tell him. He put things together for himself. He left my key on the table and walked out of the apartment. John L. ignored my calls and any efforts to make contact with him.

He eventually showed up almost a month later, still upset about the abortion. Unforgiveness brewed in his heart, but he still dealt with me while remaining in his other relationship. I never felt "second" because he was always with me. We were a family; and like clockwork, three months passed, and I was pregnant again.

Most women might agree the worst part of carrying a child is the weight gain. I'd always had a problem with being overweight and as soon as it seemed under control, I was pregnant. The difference now was the vow I made to God. No matter how things turned out, I had His full support. We were happy for a while, even if it was at the cost of someone else's pain and misery.

As the pregnancy progressed, we argued more, and he came around less. I finally felt like I was the other woman. Before the baby was born, my daughter and I moved into a three-bedroom rent house. My younger sister, Rachel, would often visit for weeks at a time.

One evening, I waited for Rachel to return my house keys she'd grabbed by mistake. Parked in the driveway, I reclined back in the seat, looked towards heaven through the sunroof and prayed to God. I was in the third trimester, big, and pregnant.

I begged God through uncontrolled tears, "Please don't let this man leave me." I couldn't face raising another child alone as a single parent. I told God, "I love him so much and I'm having his baby. Please forgive me for hurting her, but I want him."

The next weekend was Mother's Day, and he moved in with us. I believed God had answered my prayer, and we were good for a while. However, I too, was an alcoholic. I drank beer, liquor, smoked cigarettes every day, and weed occasionally, throughout the entire pregnancy.

They labeled it a high-risk pregnancy and I could only work half days as a Certified Nurse Assistant on light duty. The manager showed me some pity and allowed me to answer phones at the front desk. On June 6, 1997, John L. and I went for the last prenatal visit and it turned out I was dilating. They quickly wheeled me over to the hospital next door. We were having a baby that day. After eight to ten hours in labor, I delivered our baby girl. She weighed six pounds and was 19 inches long with a head full of coal black, wavy hair, and a cute little pie face. I'd already chosen the name Dariel. It kind of rolled off my lips one night while John L. and I watched a movie.

To people on the outside looking in, it may seem like I didn't use birth control. The pills and other contraceptives were always available, but I still got pregnant.

Chapter Three

Though an host should encamp against me, my heart shall not fear: though war should rise against me, in this will I be confident.

—Psalm 27:3

In hindsight, my life of promiscuity had it roots in an act of abuse that happened when I was about age four. I remember it as if it were yesterday.

Back then, I wore T-shirts and panties for bed at night. I didn't always have enough regular panties to last until laundry day. Often, Momma would give me toddler training pants for bed. Once I outgrew them, she'd cut slits on either side to make room for my fat thighs.

Tucked into bed with my teenage aunt, I felt safe and protected. I'd somehow rolled off the top mattress onto the box springs. The mattress and box springs were uneven, which created a nice little space and made it difficult for anyone to see me.

Now, Granddad was a local pastor who always tried to help people by sharing food or a place to stay. On this night, he brought home a distant relative, recently released from prison. Granddad didn't know I was staying over and my aunt forgot I was there. They awakened her to give up her bed for the guest. She then moved to the sofa and left me behind. Once he got in bed, he found me tucked neatly in the corner. I don't recall everything that happened that night. I do remember crawling backwards out of bed.

He said, "Pull your panties up and don't say nothing to nobody."

Terrified, I wandered through the house in the dark. I found my aunt fast asleep on the couch. I shook, trembled, and hid behind her, but I didn't mention what happened to me.

When he came out of the room, I heard all three doors creak open in the house. The first door belonged to the bedroom where Granddad directed him to sleep. The second one was in the hallway and it separated the front of the house from the back of the house. The third one was the main entry door that led outside.

I knew he was searching from me. I hid behind my auntie and peeked from a corner of the blanket. He slowly walked by, packing down the tobacco of a fresh box of Kool Filter Kings cigarettes. I waited until the door to his room was closed and made my move. I tiptoed to the kitchen and tried to get to the telephone on the wall next to the refrigerator. I called my parents, taking my finger around the dial with each digit, not making a sound. Mom answered, and I whispered for her to come and get me.

She said, "Lay down. I will come in the morning." It was ironic because my dad would always pick me up whenever I called no matter what, but not this time.

The next morning, I shared with my aunt and grandmother what happened to me and immediately, they contacted my parents. While mom took me for a checkup, dad rode around looking for the guy with his shotgun in the car. I wouldn't see him again until I was a grown woman. Even though I couldn't remember his name, that face and voice were etched in my brain.

Although the abuse was not my fault, decades later, the behavior I exhibited with males directly resulted from that long ago night. God tried to warn me to stop going down dead-end roads that led nowhere and to heed His commands. His voice could not have been any clearer than one night 25 years later.

It was a typical hot summer in Houston and the meteorologist predicted heavy rains headed our way. We went to the nearby Rice Supermarket and purchased supplies in case we lost power. We picked up snacks, a white styrofoam chest, and two candles with images of Jesus and Mother Mary. They were the only kind in the store; it seemed the entire neighborhood had the same idea. While the weather remained stable, we were preparing for the wrong storm. Our bed, night table, and the baby's bassinet were all in place. We pushed the bed against the wall and an opening to view the living room from the kitchen was above our heads. This area housed the two new candles, one in each corner.

We would have slept in the bedroom, with the air conditioning running from the living room and a fan oscillating down the hallway. In order to keep the baby comfortable, we moved the bedroom furniture into the living room to be close to the air conditioning unit because the heat made her a little fussy.

I drifted off to sleep, and I heard a distinctive voice call my name.

"Lisa." I opened my eyes in a semi-trance like state and stared at a blank white wall. The voice said, "Lisa, be free from all worldly sin and fornication, for in seven days a storm is coming."

My heart beat fast but I knew without knowing who it was that spoke to me. It was the audible voice of Almighty God!

I said to Him, "Lord, if that's you, please confirm this word."

The next morning our newborn woke me for an early morning feeding. I blundered to the kitchen, mixed a bottle, dropped it into a cup of boiling water and ran to the bathroom. I sat there with my head in hands and again the voice called my name.

"Lisa."

I raised my eyes up slowly and in this semi-trance like state, I stared at the crimson red shower curtain.

Repeating the exact message He said, "Lisa, be free from all worldly sin and fornication, for in seven days a storm is coming."

At this point, I wept uncontrollably and replied, "Yes, Lord."

He warned me of the dangers which lay ahead for all those who disobeyed Him. Needless to say, a few days passed and I no longer remembered what He said that night.

The infamous six weeks, post pregnancy, no hanky-panky orders, were now in effect and all I had in mind was being with my man. The children were both bathed, fed and tucked into bed.

We made passionate love until the sun was about to rise. Then every thought raced back. I panicked. I sat there and tried to justify what I'd done. The enemy had me focused on the close of the period and I miscounted the days and thought day seven had already passed. It was day six from the day God spoke to me. The number seven represents completion or finality. I had no clue what the seventh day would bring.

John L. was fast asleep. He faced the wall, and I fell asleep with my baby as she lay on my chest. I moved her to the middle of the bed between us. Everyone in the house was in a dead state of sleep. My dad dropped by to bring money for my mom's 50th birthday party. It would happen in a few days and we had big plans for her. He knocked at the front door and no one answered.

In my sleep I said, "Whoever that is beating on the door like the police, is about to get cussed out!" Finally, the heavy sleep released me and I screamed, "Who is it?"

"It's me!" my dad angrily barked because he had to wait a long time to get the door open. I apologized, took the money, and tucked it away in my bedroom. On the way out of that room, my voice screamed inside my head, *YO' BABY!* I ran toward the bed, down an extended hallway which seemed never ending. I made it to the living room, pulled back the covers and saw her. She was ash gray and still. She had a small drop of blood from one of her nostrils. I slightly popped the back of her pamper, but there was absolutely no movement from her. I laid her on the bed while I grabbed my glasses. I thought I looked at it wrong. I knew I wasn't seeing what I thought. I yelled her name to the top of my lungs. That woke the others.

John L. asked me, "What did you do to her?"

I screamed, "Nothing!"

I called 911 and started CPR. I had formal training, and I knew protocol, but when it's your child lying on the floor lifeless, it's a whole 'nother ball game. I needed to get to God! I wanted to bargain with Him. I realized how badly I'd messed up, but was it too late? Returning to my bedroom, I begged God to help us.

My sister who was about 19, hovered over Dariel's body with a 911 representative giving CPR instructions, as she tried to bring her back. I later discovered my six-year-old daughter stood in the doorway and watched it all unfold before her eyes. I didn't understand how God would allow this to happen to us. He's God. If He wanted to, He could change it all. I walked circles around my empty bedroom and pleaded with God to let her live. I fell to the floor and beat it with my bare hands. I screamed endlessly for Jesus to rescue me from this nightmare. The paramedics arrived and worked on her. They tried to bring her back. I was in a state of shock. John L. found me still in my bedroom, walking in circles.

"I don't have a thing to wear," I said, as if we were going to a function.

He yelled, "Just put on anything! We gotta go!"

I grabbed a wrinkled blue jean skort, paired it with a plaid pullover polo and slides. I somehow got dressed. I wanted that day to turn out differently but God did not spare us pain. This would now become my life's story.

He warned me, and I allowed the enemy to deceive me. The wages of sin is death, and someone had to pay. I believe we could not arise from sleep because the death angel was walking through the house. He selected who was ready to go, and she had completed her purpose, one week shy of two months. She was the only one prepared to leave. Those two religious candles were still in position over the bed. One was on each corner, right above my head and John L.'s head, but there wasn't a covering in the middle where she laid.

Chapter Four

One thing have I desired of the Lord, that will I seek after; that I may dwell in the house of the Lord all the days of my life, to behold the beauty of the Lord, and to enquire in his temple.
—**Psalm 27:4**

During the pregnancy with Dariel, around month six in the second trimester, I had a dream that shook me to the core. I laid down for a daily nap while on bed rest, and in a dream, I saw a baby. She was on her back with a little pink dress and matching bonnet. A skeletal face with a huge hand covered the entire tiny torso, pressed her downward into a pool of blood.

I awoke as she screamed, "Momma!"

Home alone, I trembled in fear. I thought, What in the hell was that about? None of it made any sense until after she died. I was in the place of searching and I discovered there was more to life. God walked me through this process by sharing glimpses of what was ahead. First speaking through dreams, then by audible voice. I wasn't really spiritual during the time, but I sought Him. God drew me in deeper to Himself through the love I had for the man. The relationship with John L. was complicated because he belonged to someone else. In the beginning, he treated me well, took me out on dates, paid the bills, and bought me nice things. I never intended to get caught up in a love triangle.

Once, John L. reminded me of a day when his ex-girlfriend introduced us while he waited for her in their car. I didn't remember any of that, but as he continued to talk, it all came flooding back to me.

While visiting a local convenient store, she exited the store as I entered. We embraced each other warmly because we hadn't seen each other in many years. She was always a kind person who didn't deserve to be treated this way.

We were both an only child—before my sister was born—and we quickly learned how much we had in common. We lost contact through the years but later met up in high school and picked up right where we'd left off. She and John L. dated for many years and they lived together but never married.

The day our daughter passed was dismal to say the least. I got into the ambulance with her, but the paramedics made me ride in front with the driver who happened to also be a mother. She attempted to console me by asking me to pray for my baby. It's unclear to me if she was sincere or if she was testing me to see if my grief was authentic. The ambulance made a few sudden stops.

I asked the driver, "Why can't we get to the hospital any faster?"

I was told to calm down because they had to be still while they tried to find the baby's pulse. We hadn't made it a block away from our home. It became harder to contain myself. Fear and panic overwhelmed me.

When the ambulance moved again, it seemed to travel in slow motion. We passed by the Astrodome, headed toward the Texas Medical Center.

I heard the same voice I heard previously say, "If I gave her to you now, you wouldn't want her."

We finally arrived at Texas Children's Hospital. We weren't allowed to go in to the room while the staff worked on her. They tried to revive her but she died that day, July 30, 1997. Her dad and I stood outside across from the hospital and smoked cigarettes.

Our family and friends came to check on us. Then we were told we could go in to see Dariel Antinae for the last time. Everyone went in. I was last, but honestly, I wished I didn't have to go in at all. Who wants to see their child dead?

I entered the dimly lit room. The family was there for support, but I requested that everyone leave me alone with her. They swaddled her in a blanket. I sat down in a huge rocking chair and held her in my arms.

I sang her favorite song:

> *"You are my sunshine, my other sunshine, you make me happy when skies are gray, you'll never know dear, how much mother loves you, please don't take mother's sunshine away."*

That was my version of the song and she would light up every time I sang it, but not this time. I laid her down on the bed and ran out of the room. I screamed and rushed outside to get some air. John L. held me in an effort to console me, but I was a wreck. Hospital officials came by one by one to ask us questions.

They wanted to know, "What happened to the baby?"

We didn't have any answers because we were asleep and I awakened to find her dead. It did not seem like the questions would ever end. John L. and I had another cigarette, and it poured down rain.

He said to me, "You said the storm was coming."

He referred to the weather although I was talking about this life-changing spiritual situation. A lady came out and told us to sign paperwork giving consent for an autopsy.

I said, "No," but because Dariel was a minor, they would perform one regardless of how we felt about it. Therefore, we agreed to sign the consent forms. One of the most difficult things I've ever had to do was leave the hospital without my child. We were all cried out, and it was only the first day of this ongoing nightmare.

The tragedy took a toll on all of us. We tried returning to our home, but the moment I stepped inside, every memory rushed me at once and I fell to my knees and screamed. I couldn't believe God would allow this level of pain when He had the power to prevent it all from the beginning. I had forgotten about Dariel's first doctor's visit. They diagnosed her with fetal alcohol syndrome and she appeared jaundice. The doctor ordered a lamp to lay her under for so many minutes per day. Oddly enough, the same day we returned to the house, UPS delivered the heat lamp.

I yelled at the driver, "She's dead! We don't need that anymore!"

I am remorseful but I was overwhelmed by emotions. My mom invited John L., Tina, and myself to stay with them, which ended up being a three-month visit.

The days ahead were the most grueling of all, not only because of grief but also many other emotions I experienced around the same time. This led me to an indescribable longing to feel needed. I went from fixing bottles and changing diapers to having nothing to do all in one day. Tina, now six, was left all alone to figure out this traumatic ordeal. I couldn't help her make sense of what I didn't understand. She was in first grade, dealing with severe separation anxiety. We would drop her to school and like clockwork, we'd receive a call from school officials stating they could not calm her down or that she wanted to talk to me. I couldn't see her pain for writing it off as misconduct or disrespectful behavior which warranted punishment.

She was in agony and as her mother, I missed it because of an inability to see anyone's heartache except my own. We dealt with this for quite some time until my mom suggested family prayer night. I was at a loss for what to do next. In one day, we went from being proud parents of a healthy baby girl, to a grief-stricken couple. We didn't know how to console each other because of the depth of pain we shared but neither had ever experienced.

At my parents' house, we didn't have to face the memories we avoided. We had emotions to sort through. I felt like I was on a huge wave or a roller coaster, going up and down. I felt sad, depressed, angry, and full of self-loathing guilt. Sometimes I found myself happy. These mood swings felt like a never-ending merry go round. I wanted the ride to stop and let me off, but I gripped it hard and would not let go.

One day, I cried so much it swelled my eyes almost shut. My dad was in the kitchen making breakfast one morning.

I walked up to him and asked, "Can you please help me extinguish this agonizing pain?"

He had a fork in his hand. He laid it down, turned to me, and gave me a hug.

He said, "I'm sorry, baby. I wish I could help you feel better."

He allowed me to cry on his shoulder until I eventually pulled away.

Family and friends gathered at the house every day to be with us. During that time I remained sober. I didn't want to go through that experience with a cloudy head. Each action I took came from my authentic self. My daughter deserved that much from me. I was her mother.

Don't get me wrong; thoughts raced through my mind and consumed me. I wanted to drink alcohol to numb and soothe my broken heart. Maybe it would have also quieted the voices that spoke loudly in my head. Instead, I watched everyone around me enjoy their beverages. They laughed and talked like normal. I had little to say and nothing was funny anymore.

My mind wandered to the last day I saw her. After making funeral arrangements, I'd chosen her clothes for that day. She would wear a pretty white dress, white ruffled socks with soft bottomed white shoes. I would position a matching white headband with a small pink rose on the right side of the head.

My daughters and I would all dress alike in our purity white. Her dad and her brother, Daniel, from another relationship planned to wear white buttoned-down shirts with black slacks.

Chapter Five

For in the time of trouble he shall hide me in his pavilion: in the secret of his tabernacle shall he hide me; he shall set me up upon a rock.
Psalm 27:5

The Saturday arrived for her graveside service. Fully dressed but not prepared, I sat at the edge of the bed and declared, "I'm not going."

John L. looked at me and said, "You don't have a choice."

Nothing in me could wrap my mind around what would happen in a few short minutes. Both families and all of our friends met us at the cemetery. They supported us through this difficult time.

We prepared to follow my grandfather, who was also the pastor. Daniel joined the processional. He was about to meet his sister for the first time in a cemetery on his birthday. We sat on the front row on green velvet chairs, with our feet planted on the green turf below. They set a little wooden box with a sliding lid in its place. They peeled the top back, and we saw a beautiful doll lying there, eyes closed, asleep. The crowd sighed and gasped with their hands over their open mouths. They could not believe what they witnessed. I suddenly screamed, arose from the chair and someone grabbed me. They thought I would pull her from the box. I fell to my knees in an effort to draw closer. I looked into her tiny face and sang her favorite song.

> *"You are my sunshine, my other sunshine, you make me happy when skies are gray, you'll never know dear, how much mother loves you, please don't take mother's sunshine away."*

This was the second time I sang to her and she didn't light up with a great big smile. She remained tucked in the little box cute as a button. Tears trickled down my cheeks. I wanted this to be over. The service came to a close and we proceeded to our vehicles. An old friend came over to offer condolences. She addressed me, but to this day I don't have the faintest idea what she said.

The entire time she rambled, my eyes stayed glued to the box and my baby I left behind. If they all would've left me alone, I would've remained to see her properly tucked into her new home. My old friend noticed I didn't pay her any attention and she figured out what I was looking at. Later, I forced my body into the car. We drove away and left her again, this time in a little box forever.

Weeks passed after that life-changing tragedy, and in an effort to move forward, I enrolled in medical billing/

coding classes. Nothing could replace my daughter, but I knew I had to live my life.

One day while in a lecture, I received a page from an unknown number. I returned the call around lunchtime in the college cafeteria. An unfamiliar voice picked up. The man on the other end was from the homicide division and he declared they ruled my baby's death as SIDS (Sudden Infant Death Syndrome). Relieved is an understatement because on top of the grief, our fate rested in the hands of man. We weren't guilty of anything, but it was a relief to know that someone else saw our genuine innocence.

Right after her death, homicide detectives had demanded entry into the house where she died. We watched from outside through an open door, and witnessed them take her pacifier, sample an almost empty bottle of milk, and test the fresh formula already mixed in the refrigerator.

Many heartbroken moms may agree our daily mission is to fill the gaping hole in our hearts. I tried desperately to replace that missing piece of me that died with her. I aggressively attacked John L. every night for sex, determined to make another baby.

A few months later, things greatly changed between us as the grief took its toll and we grew further apart. I was pregnant again, and that didn't help our situation, it only added more pressure. We were grief stricken with a rocky relationship. We faced financial difficulties, and now we had a baby on the way. I felt a bit overwhelmed and I checked around for inexpensive abortion clinics to relieve the burden. I didn't give thought to the promise I'd made to God.

My cousin, Shaun, who was also pregnant, asked for a ride to her doctor's visit. She introduced her OB/GYN as the best doctor for high-risk pregnancy. She asked if they could test me and they agreed. I'd already taken an at home pregnancy test but I wanted to be sure. Needless to say it was positive and after I completed the paperwork, her doctor became my OB/GYN.

That confirmation made me sad because of the ups and downs of my relationship with John L., however, Shaun seemed overjoyed. I didn't understand her happiness and begged her not to tell the family. We walked into the house and she blurted out all she knew. Now she could block me from getting rid of the baby as I'd shared with her. I thought, *How can I do this now that everyone knows I'm pregnant?* Feeling stuck, afraid, and a little betrayed, this new person grew inside of me and there was nothing I could do about it.

I pleaded with God, and I believed with all my heart that God would somehow give my daughter back. Nobody could persuade me otherwise. Around the second trimester, I was taking a mid-day nap when the phone rang. Shaun was on the line and she wanted to connect me with another cousin's wife, Nikki, who said it was urgent that we speak. I took the call, and I listened as she shared the vision God gave her regarding the child in my womb. She stated that she did not see herself as a prophet, but God showed her something that must be released. She said after dropping her husband off to work, a vision flooded her mind. According to her, it was so vivid, she could no longer see to drive. Nikki prophesied the child I carried was a boy and that he'd grow up to be a bishop in the church.

The conversation infuriated me. I couldn't believe they'd woke me up with "this mess."

I dismissed it by saying, "God told me I'm having another girl. Thank you and goodbye."

Later, I found out I was having a boy. It crushed me to the core, and I've never admitted to Nikki I was wrong.

The physical confrontations between John L. and I became more intense, and the stress was too much to bear. I had to argue and fight although I was big and pregnant.

It turned out John L. was battling his own demons of alcoholism and drug addiction. He'd already moved out of the house we once shared but he never stopped coming over to interrogate my life. He lived between his mom's and another woman's house, but he said he loved me. No longer willing to put up with his abusive actions, I pushed him away. John L. wanted to live his life with the other woman while controlling mine. I expected more from him than he could give. Escalating conflict between us sent Tina and I packing. We left home to spend time with my cousin, Walter, and his family, just for some peace.

One night I went to shower, and I noticed blood running down my legs. I felt pressure in my lower abdomen. I sat on the toilet and thought I needed to do number two. When I pushed, something fell into the bowl and made quite a splash. When I got up, I saw blood everywhere, along with something else that floated in the commode.

I screamed for Walter's wife, Felecia, and she ran in the bathroom, with her eyes bucked in terror. I showed her what came out of me. She retrieved some old tongs from the kitchen and a zip locked storage bag. I stood there in disbelief. When she pulled it from the bowl, it looked like an early stage embryo, the one from the development charts which resembles an alien in the second month.

While disinfecting the bathroom, she said, "Get cleaned up. We are going to the hospital."

We trashed the tongs but carried the zip locked bag with us to the ER. The doctor saw it but didn't seem to recognize it, although he tried to explain it away. I thought it may have been a miscarried fraternal twin, but no one ever confirmed my suspicions. After this episode, the OB/GYN put me on total bed rest and admitted me into the hospital for a procedure called the McDonald Cerclage. It is a common technique used to stitch the upper part of the cervix while the lower part has effaced. They remove it prior to delivery.

Shortly after, I dreamed my baby boy was born, and the nurse wheeled him into the room from the nursery, but I had turned my back to the baby. Without looking to see, I asked, "What's the gender?"

She said, "It's a boy."

He was so pretty, I knew he was a girl. In disbelief, I pulled back the covers to check the genitalia. He was a boy. Before I could turn my back again, I saw our baby girl who died. She descended through the ceiling, on her side, with her head facing me. We made eye contact. She smiled at me and laid her body down inside of my newborn son. What a connection. It was so detailed, I knew it was a message from God. He didn't allow her to come back as herself, but He created her a new body and the baby I saw vividly in the dream, is the son who was later born to me.

Chapter Six

And now shall mine head be lifted up above mine enemies round about me: therefore will I offer in his tabernacle sacrifices of joy; I will sing, yea, I will sing praises unto the Lord.

—**Psalm 27:6**

The high-risk nature of the pregnancy drove Tina and I back to my parents' house for a while. The on again, off again relationship with John L. had gotten old to both he and I, and we neared an end.

I returned to my parents' house after a day of shopping for the arrival of our new baby. I rushed into the bathroom, sat down, with a phone in hand, and it rang. John L. called to check on us, but I was angry because I hadn't heard from him all day. I didn't know he'd called my parents' house a few times while I was out shopping. John L. was always angry when he didn't know my whereabouts. He figured he was supposed to know my every move, or it meant I was cheating on him. His level of jealousy became quite disturbing, but I often dismissed the paranoia because of his addictive behavior.

I hung up the phone and washed my hands. Suddenly there was a big gush and water poured down my legs. I immediately picked up the phone and frantically tried to call him back, but he wouldn't take my calls. I stuck my head out the bathroom door and yelled for my dad. He ran toward the bathroom door, eyes bucked in fear.

"Don't panic," I said, "but my water just broke and I need to get to the hospital."

My sister and mom were at work and Tina was in school. I quickly showered and grabbed the overnight bag already prepared for this day.

My dad dropped me off at the hospital and said, "Your mom is on the way from work to be with you and I'll get Tina after school."

I checked into the hospital and was escorted to a room at once. Mom showed up not long after my doctor came by to examine me. The contractions drew closer, and the pain declared labor would soon follow. They prepped me and wheeled me into the operating room. Once our son was born, the doctor would perform a tubal ligation as planned. I felt nothing after they injected something into my IV. It was lights out.

I don't know how much time had passed, but I peeked out from behind my eyelids and looked down toward my feet. I asked them, "What are y'all waiting for?"

The doctor and my mom looked back at me and said in unison, "We're waiting on you to push!"

I couldn't stay awake because of the intravenous drugs coursing through my body. I continued to fall back asleep.

My baby's heart rate dropped. He was stuck in a weird position as he came through the birthing canal. The doctor used forceps and tugged on his head to guide his way. After some time, he made it; all 8 pounds, 10 ounces and 22 inches of him. Officially the prophecy regarding the gender had come to pass. I had hoped everyone else was wrong.

The next day, visitors awakened me. John L. and his mom had stopped by to see the baby we named D.J. I felt like he brought her along to see if D.J. was his baby. That's one of the ways some people verify fatherhood in our culture. The mother looks the baby over to confirm whether or not the baby belongs to their family. At least that's the thought behind that foolish process.

She took one look at our son, then looked at John L. and nodded her head in approval. I never said a word because I knew who he belonged to. In your knowing of the truth, there is no need to argue over what you already know.

In time, they discharged me from the hospital. We found ourselves back at my parents' house. This was an enormous difference from bringing our baby girl home. To be honest, it terrified us to go home. It seemed like family and friends weren't as excited to visit him. We received a few calls now and then to see how we were doing. It felt like they were protecting their hearts after becoming closely attached to the little girl who left us. Instead of the two girls I once had, now I have a girl and a boy.

This new addition to the family wasn't without alarming moments. D.J. had episodes in the middle of the night when he would suddenly stop breathing. Paramedics came and escorted us to the nearest Children's Hospital. They diagnosed him with NSIDS. (Near Sudden Infant Death Syndrome).

They detained us for overnight observation. The next morning, they sent us home with a device to monitor him while he slept. After they realized the history of a sibling with SIDS, they were adamant that he should wear it. The moment he stopped breathing, a loud alarm would sound and wake everyone in the house.

Eventually, we returned to our home to put our lives back together. This time it was only me and my children. It felt strange being the protector over the house. I was used to having John L. there. I never before thought about home security.

When I mentioned this to my dad, he reluctantly gave me his 22 caliber pistol.

"It is only for protection!" he repeated.

He knew I could be a hothead at times and didn't want me to get into trouble by having a gun.

My cousin, Walter, his wife, Felecia, and their two children came to stay with us for a while. I'd asked them to come stay with us because I was uncomfortable at home, and it made me feel better to have others around. I willingly gave up my bedroom to them and I slept on the couch.

Late one night, everyone, in the house, including myself was fast asleep. There was a loud knock at the door.

"Boom! Boom! Boom!"

I sprung to my feet like a cat and ran to the bedroom to get the gun. I jumped on the bed where my cousin and his wife were asleep. I attempted to look through a tall window over the bed. They woke up with me almost standing on their heads and tried to figure out what I was doing.

I screamed and said, "Somebody's beating on the door like they wanna get in here!"

I gave Walter the gun, and he went to check things out. He walked outside. He stealthily went around the entire house, but he didn't find anything, neither did he see anything out of place.

Back inside, he turned to me and asked, "What's wrong with you?"

I said, "I promise I heard somebody beating at the door. Somebody was out there!"

Walter and Felecia returned to bed, while I safely put away the gun. I walked through the hallway and went back to the sofa to lie down.

A voice said, "Lisa it's Me knocking on the door of your heart. When are you going to let me in?"

Hearing these words stopped me in my tracks. I fell to my knees in the center of the living room and I cried out for help. I asked God to please forgive me and help me. Nothing in my life made sense anymore. I felt like I was losing it, and changing my ways was the only thing left to do.

I wanted to change for real this time and walk in a new Christian life, but I did not realize what it took to be delivered from all of my issues. I had accepted Jesus Christ into my heart as Lord and Savior of my life at age 12. He always had His hooks in me and now He was reeling me back into a relationship with Him.

I repented of all the sins I'd committed to detour my life on the wrong course. I starved for hope and love, and I drew nearer to God. I studied the Bible, attended church services, spent time in prayer and fasting. It made a tremendous difference. God began to guide my life in a more positive direction. I walked away from old friends and He forced me to put down old habits, while He healed my broken heart and helped me to forgive myself and others.

I desperately wanted to find another job. I frantically prayed for one.

As I drove away from an interview, I heard the Lord say, "If you want a career, put down the weed." He knew that every suitable work environment required a urinalysis. That was only the beginning of my process. I landed a career in the healthcare industry as a medical biller and insurance collector. I'd been there for quite some time when my son became ill with a fever. I called out from work that day and stayed in bed with my children. I didn't make a lot of money back then, and I was reluctant to ask the children's dads for help. I relied on my parents for assistance. My dad dropped off medicine for D.J. who was then about 1 ½ years old.

The pediatrician's office suggested alternating between Tylenol and Motrin to break his fever. I had administered the first dose because something elevated the fever. I sat up in bed with my son lying asleep next to me. His body jerked uncontrollably. His eyes rolled back into his head, as his face turned blue and foam ran from his mouth.

I wondered if the house was haunted and if some evil spirit was after my children? It was a random thought, but I wondered about it. The phone company had disconnected my telephone that day for non-payment. I sent my daughter to use the neighbor's phone to call 911 for help.

I brought him into the living room, laid him on the floor and put my two fingers into his mouth to secure his tongue. I knew better than to put my fingers in the mouth of someone having a seizure, but at that moment, him breathing was all that mattered.

I screamed to the top of my lungs, "YOU CAN'T HAVE NO MORE OF MY BABIES!"

D.J. bit down on my index and middle fingers so hard, I felt his teeth near the bone. In pain, I held that position and I didn't move until the paramedics arrived.

Chapter Seven

Hear, O Lord, when I cry with my voice: have mercy also upon me, and answer me.

—Psalm 27:7

The neighbor walked Tina home with her cordless phone in hand. She allowed me to call my mom to let her know what was happening. Of course she was frantic.

I later found out Tina was outside on the driveway bargaining with God while they worked on him. She begged God not to take her little brother. She offered herself instead. I figured this was her way to escape from having to experience the trauma all over. She would rather give him an opportunity to live than endure the death of another sibling. I know I couldn't bear the thought of the death of another child.

When my mom arrived, she ran inside, saw D.J. on the floor surrounded by paramedics who worked feverishly on him. It devastated her.

She yelled, "What happened?"

I couldn't answer the question because I didn't know myself, but upon hearing our exchange of words, one paramedic blurted out, "It looks like a febrile seizure."

We looked at one another because we had never heard of that before.

He explained, "It's when a fever gets too high, too fast."

I asked, "Will he be all right?"

He replied, "He'll recover. This is the third one we've seen this week."

There was a sigh of relief because we weren't sure of what we were about to face. My daughter went with my mom and I climbed into the ambulance, headed for the hospital. The doctor got him stabilized. The fever became under control and they discharged us with prescriptions. What a day. All I could do was thank God for not taking him away from me.

******

Undoubtedly, over the years, we've had some rough patches, storms and turbulence, but through it all God has become the center of my world. I never knew love so faithful, forgiving, long-suffering and painful. Some may say that statement doesn't flow because our God is loving and kind. Yes, He is that and much more, but I've experienced pain He's allowed through my disobedience.

I have learned the word of God which declares, "All things work together for the good of them who love God and who are the called according to His purpose" (Romans 8:28).

All means all and yes, He'll even mix in pain if it'll work out for our good. He didn't say it would feel good to us, but it will ultimately be good for us.

God alone has brought me to the place where I am today. I've come through extremely difficult circumstances to become who I am: a strong, confident, woman of God, filled with His love and integrity.

The struggle as a single mother was real. I endured the abortions because I never wanted a lot of children. The hard truth is, I was laying down making babies that I didn't want and couldn't take care of. I can't change what I've done in the past, I can only look ahead to a better future.

The heartache of such a loss was intense. I didn't think I'd ever get past that hard place in life. It's been over 23 years and it's still painful at times, but not like in the beginning. Tears well up whenever I try to picture my daughter all grown up; how she'd speak, walk, and carry herself. I mark special milestones along the way as a memorial of her high school prom, graduation, and marriage ceremonies. I will never have an opportunity of knowing those events, but as life moves forward, she'll always live on in my heart.

After six years of a rocky, strained relationship, John L. and I got married in 2002. God delivered us from alcohol and drug addictions, and through our individual healing processes we overcame our abusive, destructive past. We're older, more reserved, and still going strong after eighteen years of marriage. The children are all grown up and we now get to spoil the grandchildren.

I've been on a committed course to serve God and His people in ministry for many years. In this season, He's impressed upon my heart to share some of my personal journey.

Maybe in the future I'll be able to share more because there is a lot left unsaid but until then this is my story. Be encouraged by seeking God with all your heart, release every struggle over to Him and watch things change. My reality is, I aborted three and God took one away from me (3:1). He told me to write this book because someone needed to know, it doesn't matter what you've done, God can still use you.

Grief Resources and SIDS Prevention Page

1. healgrief.org
2. firstcandle.org
3. compassionatefriends.org
4. dougy.org
5. childrengrieve.org
6. cdc.gov
7. healthychildren.org
8. nichd.nih.gov
9. sidsamerica.org
10. Grief Hotline 1-800-221-7437

October: SIDS Awareness Month

October 15th: Pregnancy and Infant Loss Remembrance Day

About the Author

Apostle E.C. Friar is a 52-year-old wife, mother, and grandmother from Houston, Texas. She attended Houston Public Schools and graduated from Evan E. Worthing High School May, 1986. She spent two years pursuing a degree in Nursing at Prairie View A&M University in Prairie View, Texas. After moving back to Houston, she began a career in the Healthcare Industry as a Certified Nurse Assistant.

Apostle Friar accepted the call to spread the Gospel in December 2004, and preached her first sermon in January 2005. Approximately six years later, God instructed her to establish a church in the

Houston area. She would then become installed as the Founder/Senior Pastor of Give God Glory Ministries.

UT MD Anderson Cancer Center employed her from 2007 to 2019 as a Clinical Billing Specialist in the Division of Anesthesiology & Critical Care. While managing family, ministry, and career, she returned to college at age 42. She obtained a Bachelor's of Science Degree in Health Administration and Health Management at the University of Phoenix, Houston Campus. She is currently in full-time ministry. Apostle Friar is faithfully committed to serving God and His people. The mission is to fulfill the call of God by eliminating the complexity of the Gospel. The message is clear, so all who hear may receive Jesus Christ as Lord and Savior.

In Loving Memory of

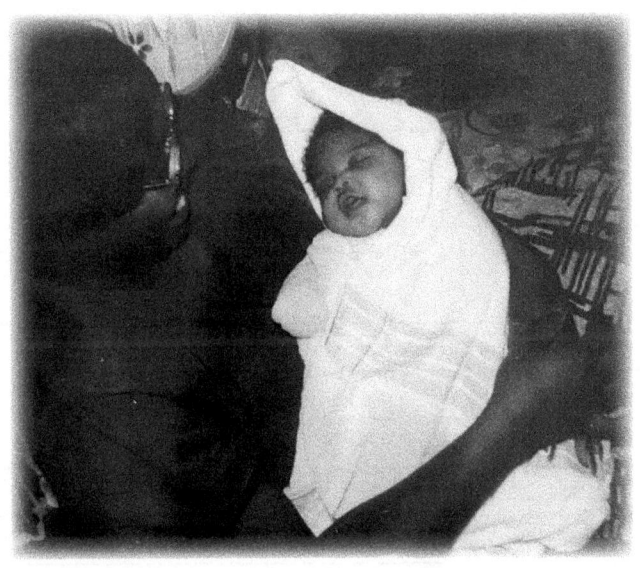

Dariel Antinae Friar

Alpha June 6, 1997 - Omega July 30, 1997

Takeaways